August 5 1978

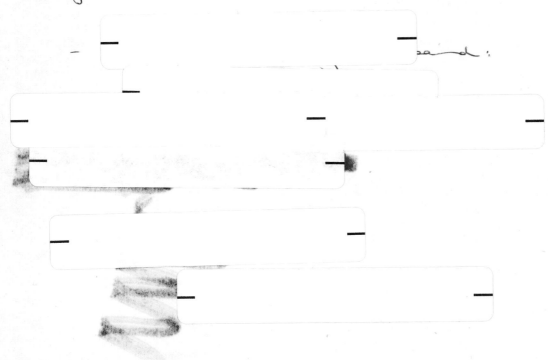

Spitfire SPECIAL

TED HOOTON

Paintings by M. Roffe

London

IAN ALLAN LTD

EVERY PICTURE TELLS A STORY . . .

The aircraft on the cover and that shown above are the same aircraft: Spitfire Mark VB, AD233. The photo above shows AD233 in green-grey camouflage as it appeared fresh off the Castle Bromwich production line in September, 1941. Photographed with ortho film, the yellow outline of the fuselage roundel appears to be black, but noteworthy is the black spinner and also the lack of fuselage tail-band.

Shortly afterwards the aircraft was ferried to No 37 MU, Burtonwood, where it would have had the white spinner and tail-band added (presumably due to a lack of the regulation duck-egg blue paint). Since the serial number was now obscured by the tail-band it was repeated on the top of the fin in small digits. Also, at this time, a TR1143 VHF radio would have been fitted and, with this, the small 'prong' on the aerial mast would have been removed.

Allocated to No 222 Squadron at North Weald on October 1, 1941, it was occasionally flown on operations by Sqn Ldr H. T. Gilbert during November and December. During the Christmas period the aircraft was partly resprayed, and the cover photo shows that the presentation name 'WEST BORNEO I' was covered over on the starboard side of the fuselage, but was probably retained on the port side.

On January 19, 1942, another ex-Battle of Britain pilot, Sqn Ldr R. M. Milne DFC (with eleven enemy aircraft to his credit), took command of 222 Squadron and, on March 8, he adopted AD233 as his personal aircraft—as shown by the pennant, which would have been repeated on the port side. Until May 22, when Sqn Ldr J. S. Jankiewicz replaced Milne, the latter flew the aircraft on many operational sorties over Northern France, and the cover photo shows the aircraft during that period. Yet another famous pilot flew AD233 when, on May 7, the North Weald Wing Leader, Wg Cdr F. D. S. Scott-Malden DFC, borrowed the aircraft (in place of AB202, his normal 'mount') for an operation.

Finally, on May 25, 1942, 'Rodeo No 51', an operation over Ostend was laid on, and Jankiewicz on his first sortie with 222 Squadron, was to lead the Wing in AD233. However, over Gravelines a large force of Fw190's jumped the Spitfires and, since AD233 did not return, Jankiewicz was posted as missing . . .

Cover and title page photos by Charles E. Brown

Contents

First published 1972
Third impression 1975
Fourth impression 1977
ISBN 07110 0293 2
Code: DX/0277

Printed and published in the United Kingdom by
Ian Allan Ltd., Shepperton, Middlesex

Opposite: Of a similar standard to the Spitfire used for the first high-speed diving tests, the PR. Mark XI above, EN654, demonstrates the manoeuvrability of the Spitfire as it executes a roll away from the photographic aircraft.

AUTHOR'S NOTE

This is an offshoot of the excellent Airscene series started by Philip Moyes. I must express my appreciation to him in allowing me to intrude on his well-established picture-book format, and also to G. Freeman Allen of Ian Allan in giving me a free hand.

In attempting a special on the Spitfire and Seafire, there is a great danger in repeating the efforts of previous compilers and authors in this field. Therefore, I have tried very hard to present fresh new material and photographs. In this, an attempt has been made to provide historians, modellers, and the casual reader, with both interesting and detailed information. Since 'one picture is worth a thousand words', the photographs have been carefully chosen, and because brisk captions do not always complete the picture, some effort has been taken to fill in the details of each aircraft photograph or painting.

I would especially like to thank Michael Roffe for his excellent paintings; also my entire family for proof reading, map making, assistance in photographic searches, and in showing patience during many silent hours of research and writing! I hope readers will enjoy this publication as much as I have in putting it together.

ACKNOWLEDGEMENTS

I wish to thank the entire staff of the Air Historical Branch (RAF), Ministry of Defence, for allowing me to delve into the official records which were so useful in the preparation of this booklet. Any views or observations relating to the official material used, are mine and do not necessarily reflect those of the Ministry. Also, I wish to acknowledge the assistance of the staff of the Imperial War Museum who provided many of the photos and were so patient in my searches.

Thanks are also due to Bill Aston, Peter Arnold, Roy Cross, Dr Halliday of the National Physical Laboratory, Robert von Knorring, Wg Cdr McClure, Jo Ottley, Derek Perry, Derek Reed, and Flt Lt Watton for help received; and the following for photographs: Chris Ashworth, Len Bachelor, Margaret Barlaup of Norsk Telegrambyra, Charles E. Brown, Major Brycker of Flygvapnet, Public Archives of Canada, Canada Wide Photos, T.P.M. Cooper-Slipper, Cdr I.J. Davis RN, Salih Evren of the Turkish Air Force, *Flight International,* F.G. Freeman Jr, J. Guthrie, Bob Hedger, Les Hunt, Junior Chamber of Commerce Southampton, J. Oughton, Don Reid, United States Air Force, and Vickers-Armstrongs.

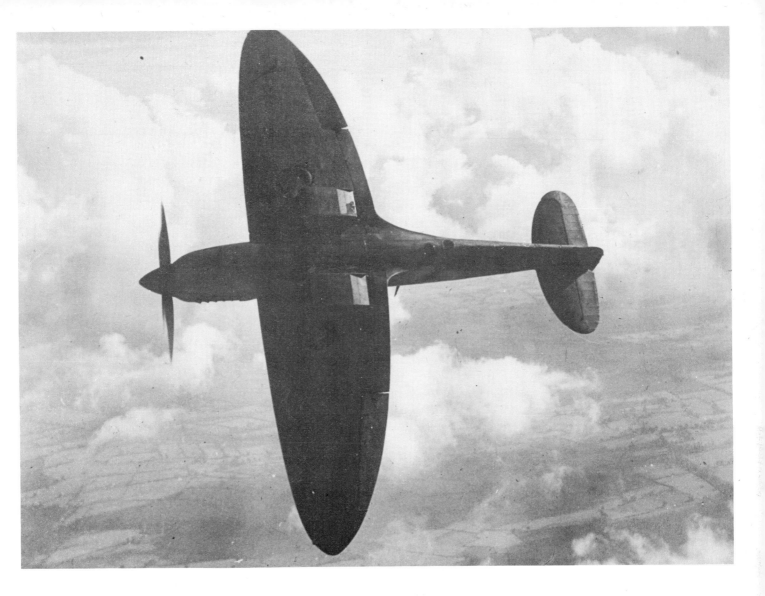

Performance and versatility—the Hallmark of the Spitfire

By the year 1943 during World War II, many pilots flying fighter aircraft in Britain and the USA had experienced loss of control of their aircraft when diving at high speeds. It became apparent that serious investigation was needed and, in September, the Royal Aircraft Establishment began a series of special flight tests to investigate the effects of compressibility. The scientific testing of aircraft at speeds close to that of sound was a new field of investigation and required the right technical approach, an above-average test pilot, and the right aircraft.

It is therefore no surprise to learn that the aircraft chosen for these tests was the Spitfire. The test pilot who was to carry out the majority of the early flights was S/L Alan Martindale, and the civilian project officer was John Charnley. The work that they were to do in the succeeding year was to be of very great significance, as well as proving the astonishing performance of the Spitfire.

A Mark PR.XI, EN409, was chosen for the tests, and within a few months the phenomenal diving speed of 620mph had been reached. This speed corresponds to a Mach number of 0.92 of the speed of sound (M = 1.0). Later, Martindale was killed in another aircraft during the tests (due to a propeller failure), and F/L Mair carried on with the work in another Spitfire XI, PL827, with speeds up to 0.85 Mach as a regular occurrence.

What was so remarkable about these flights was that no other piston-engined aircraft ever reached such speeds and, until the advent of the F-86 Sabre in 1947-48, no jet aircraft could match the Spitfire in diving speed.

By 1943 the Spitfire was at the peak of its development. It was in service in all the climatic regions of the world as an interceptor fighter, an offensive fighter-bomber, a carrier-borne fighter, and for photographic-reconnaissance. Some versions could fight at altitudes of 45,000 feet, others could fly for six hours in sorties of well over a thousand miles. Its versatility was unmatched, and clearly it was the result of a man of genius: R. J. Mitchell.

1934 to 1941—Design, Early Development and Into Battle

Above: The first production Spitfire I, K9787, at the A&AEE Martlesham Heath, for type trials, in the late summer of 1938. This aircraft was fitted with a 'wire cage' rudder guard at the top of the fin. This was installed to prevent the cable of the anti-spin parachute fouling the rudder at the horn-balance. It was fitted to a number of early aircraft (including those of 19 Squadron) and was not an aerial for IFF Mk. I, as has been suggested elsewhere. IFF was not fitted to Spitfires until late in 1940.

Opposite: The adaptability of the Spitfire is well illustrated by these two photographs taken almost twelve years apart. At the top is the Spitfire prototype, K5054, as it first appeared at Eastleigh in March 1936; below is a production Seafire FR.47 in early 1948. Not only are the external changes in the airframe quite apparent, but also the handling characteristics had changed out of all recognition over the years. Even so, the Seafire 47 was very popular in the Royal Navy.
There are also several interesting points to note in these two aircraft. K5054 is in its original form with integral fin and large rudder horn balance. What is not so obvious, is the shape of the radiator: in its early stages the leading edge of the intake was canted forward so that, in the plan view, it followed the angle of the undercarriage cut-out in the wing.
The Seafire, VP447, later served with 800 Squadron of the Fleet Air Arm aboard HMS *Triumph* in the Far East and, in late 1949, was based at Sembawang, Singapore, for anti-bandit strikes in Malaya.

In looking back at historical events it is often possible to pick out certain periods of time that were very significant in their effect on the course of history. Prior to the Second World War, the summer months of 1934 were just such a time, in terms of both political events and the development of military aviation.

Politically, there was unrest, assassination, and uncertainty in Europe. In Germany, Hitler, who had risen to power in the previous year, was carrying out the bloody purges of the Nazi party. The Chancellor of Austria was assassinated, and Hitler and Mussolini had met for the first time. In England, a wave of pacifism was still being felt, although the Facist Party was now seen to be a focal point for violence, and the public were beginning to feel slightly uneasy. The International Disarmament Conference had been adjourned indefinitely and in Parliament, the first RAF Expansion Scheme was announced, although rather apologetically, since no extra money was voted for the purpose.

In aviation, the American aircraft industry had led the way since 1930 with the development of civil transport and bomber monoplanes. The Lockheed Orion in 1931, with its smooth lines and retractable undercarriage had influenced the design of the Heinkel He70 and the Airspeed Courier in Europe. Boeing's work on stressed-skin metal construction had advanced the state-of-the-art and, in

Above: April 1940, and Spitfire I, P9450, shows the production standard and markings of the period. Most noticeable features are the tapered aerial mast (replacing the earlier 'stick' type) and the addition of an external armoured windscreen. This aircraft went to 64 Squadron at Kenley, was damaged during the Battle of Britain, and was afterwards converted to a Mark VA.

Right: By the winter of 1939-40 production of the Spitfire had got into its stride and this Mark I, L1090, of the first production batch, could be spared for evaluation in Canada, where this photo was taken. It returned to the UK in August, 1940.

Right: The Type 330 Spitfire III was designed during the winter of 1938-39 as the successor to the Marks I and II. It first flew in the late spring of 1940 and, although it was never produced in quantity, it laid the foundation for the development of the later versions of the Marks V, VII, VIII, and IX.

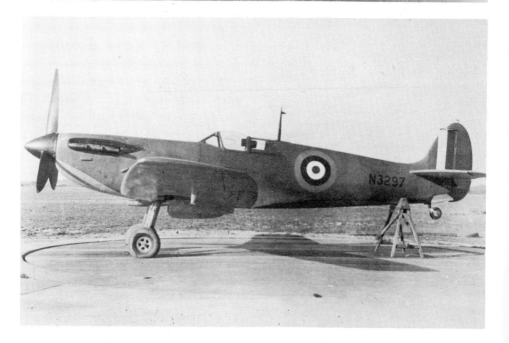

Opposite: Using a basic airframe similar to the Mark III was the original Type 337 Spitfire IV, designed in the autumn of 1939 to take the Griffon engine which was developed by Rolls-Royce, beginning in January of that year. Due to the priorities of the Battle of Britain, the first prototype, DP845 shown here, was not ordered until May 1941. When the photo-reconnaissance Mark VD was re-allocated as the PR.IV, DP845 was then renamed as the Spitfire F.20. It is shown here in that form in 1942.

the summer of 1934, the Douglas DC-2 had entered airline service.

Coupled with this development in transport aircraft, there was the impetus provided by the Schneider Trophy races which had culminated in the attainment of a speed of over 400mph in 1931. The most significant trend in the Schneider racers was the attention to streamlining, the need for low-frontal area in-line engines, and new fuel mixtures.

In 1934 the political events in Europe, and the new technology, were to influence the design of military fighter aircraft. In Germany, the Messerschmitt Bf109 was beginning to take shape on the drawing boards, while the first Heinkel He51 biplane fighters were being delivered to the then-secret Luftwaffe. In Russia the new Polikarpov I-17 monoplane fighter was being built, and the French Armée de l'Air issued a fighter specification which was to result in the Morane 405 and the Bloch 151.

In Britain, the RAF was very weak, with only thirteen squadrons of biplane fighters, and an experimental acoustic early-warning system that was to subsequently prove almost useless. New fighter aircraft for the RAF were still very far away, as the competition for a type to meet the F.7/30 specification was dragging on. In June 1934, the Bristol 133 appeared—the first British fighter to have a retractable undercarriage—but it was to crash the following year. The Rolls-Royce Goshawk engine had been a failure, and the new PV-12 engine (later to be named the Merlin) had failed its first 100 hour test.

In view of all these political and aeronautical events, it is not surprising that there was a flurry of memoranda and meetings at the Air Ministry at that time. This activity led to three very important developments: the requirement for a really advanced fighter design; the need for an eight-gun armament; and the beginnings of an idea that was to become RDF—the radar early-warning and control system.

At Vickers-Supermarine, R.J. Mitchell, worried by political events and already a sick man, had been engaged in design studies of new fighter aircraft since late 1933 as a result of dissatisfaction with his own F.7/30 design. Further stimulation was provided by the F.5/34 specification in February 1934, but in July of that fateful year he began the design of the Supermarine Type 300, later to be named the Spitfire.

It is interesting to note that in the period from 1934 to 1935 over twenty comparable types of single-seat fighters were designed in eight different countries. Of these contempories of the Type 300, only one, the Bf109, incorporated the advanced features which led to the ultimate success and development potential of the Spitfire.

In designing the aircraft there is no doubt that Mitchell incorporated all the lessons of streamlining that he had learnt from the Schneider racers; the retractable undercarriage was as simple as that on his earlier Walrus design, and American developments in construction certainly influenced him. He chose the Goshawk engine originally, intending to have a retractable radiator under the starboard wing, and flush-mounted oil tank under the nose, cooled by the airflow. These items were to change when the Merlin replaced the Goshawk, but the outstanding feature of the design was the wing. His choice of the new NACA 2200 aerofoil section, coupled with the low-drag elliptical shape, was the stroke of genius.

It has been suggested that Mitchell was inspired by the design of the Heinkel He70, but this is simply not correct. In 1930 he had designed the Type 179 flying boat with a wing almost identical to that of the Type 300. For the flying boat, his choice may well have been influenced by the 1926 wind-tunnel tests of the Short-Bristow Crusader at the National Physical Laboratory. The Crusader was intended for the 1927 Schneider Race, and had a very graceful elliptical wing which gave excellent low-drag characteristics.

In the summer of 1934, Mitchell's design and the Air Ministry's new ideas coincided, and it is to the credit of the Air Staff that events moved quickly afterwards. In January 1935 the Type 300 was ordered to Specification

Above: This shows a Spitfire IIA of 65 Squadron at Tangmere early in 1941. The presentation marking has now changed to that of the 'East India Squadron' and has been somewhat embellished. This aircraft, YT-C was P7856 (not P7850 as reported elsewhere) and, subsequently, had a long career, serving in 616, 412, 310, 416 Squadrons and on operational training until 1945.

Left: This shows the starboard side of YT-D, R6799, and the original form of the 'East India' marking. The group includes Sqn Ldr Sawyer (in the cockpit), and Captain H. H. Balfour, The Under Secretary of State for Air.

Top Left: Photos of genuine 'Battle of Britain' Spitfires are somewhat rare, and this picture is both interesting and yet rather sad. Taken on July 15, 1940 it shows a line-up of 65 Squadron Mk.IA aircraft at Hornchurch. On this day, these eight new aircraft had been formally presented to 'A' flight to form 'The East India Fund Flight'. It would appear that there was a deliberate attempt, at the time, to mislead the Germans about our rate of production and the censor has deleted the serial of YT-D. However it is now known that this was, in fact, R6799. The aircraft is painted in the colours of the period, green and brown, and the new duck-egg blue undersides, with no roundel. It has HF radio, but no IFF wire aerial between the fuselage and tailplane.
R6799 was flown operationally by Sqn Ldr H. C. Sawyer during the following days but, tragically, he was killed in this aircraft on the night of August 2, when taking off for a night patrol.

F.37/34 as an experimental eight-gun fighter. There was some pressure to place a production order in the spring of 1935 but this was resisted and, in March 1936, the prototype Spitfire made its first flight.

During that month the Germans re-occupied the Rhineland, the Bf109 was ordered into production, and in Parliament the Air Estimates were doubled to allow over £50 million for RAF expansion. The Air Staff who had hoped the original F.5/34 specification would produce the new RAF fighter, now recognised the Spitfire (and Hawker Hurricane) as being superior and, in June 1936, the two fighters were ordered. The Spitfire order was for 310 aircraft to Specification 16/36, issued on July 28.

Production of the Spitfire was very slow at first. It was the first aircraft to be built from components sub-contracted from outside the parent firm, and Supermarine had no experience of building such large numbers of aircraft. Not only did they have the Spitfire but they were building Stranraer and Walrus flying-boats at the same time. Also, until the spring of 1938, there was no priority in allocating resources needed for the vast expansion schemes. The first production Spitfire appeared in May 1938, but production did not really get into its stride until February 1939.

As the aircraft entered service in August 1938, and in the months that followed, it is quite apparent that the qualities of the Spitfire were not fully appreciated by the general public, nor by some elements within the RAF.

Spitfire 1A, SD-J X4381, of 501 Squadron at Colerne, June 1941.
With the exception of the duck-egg blue spinner and fuselage band,
it is in its original production colours of late August 1940. These
include the tall fin flash (on all Spitfires until December 1940.
and retained on aircraft built prior to that date), and small
underwing roundel at the tip—which was peculiar to the X42 to
X44 series. This X batch of aircraft were part of the production
subterfuge at the time. They had only been ordered a few months
before their production began in mid-July 1940, and interrupted
the R batch at R7022. The latter batch were resumed at R7023
in January 1941.

The Hurricane had entered service before the Spitfire and
the publicity made it appear as though the former was the
faster aircraft. The development potential of the Spitfire
was not yet apparent, and manoeuvrability in combat
was still thought to be of paramount importance by many.
In April 1940, comparative tests between a Spitfire,
Curtiss H-75, and Gloster F.5/34 (both design contempories), produced the rather startling report that the
Spitfire was '. . . more suitable . . . for intercepting high-
speed bombers', and 'for combat . . . the Curtiss is superior'.
These thoughts were somewhat modified in early May
when comparative tests were run between a captured
Bf109E, and a Spitfire I; the former was judged to be a
'formidable opponent'. This opinion was soon confirmed
over Dunkirk, when fifteen of the nineteen Spitfire squad-
tons of Fighter Command were committed to battle against
the Luftwaffe, and met the Bf109 in combat for the first
time.

During May 1940 the first signs of the adaptability of
the Spitfire became apparent when the Norwegian
campaign resulted in the first float-plane version (the
Type 342 with Blackburn Roc floats, and also the Type

344 design project with Supermarine floats). Another
design panic at this time was the Type 343 long-range
version with external fuel tanks on the wing. All of these
projects were too late for service in Norway, and were not
needed for the Battle of Britain which now began.

It is not proposed to describe the activities of the Spitfire
during the Battle as these have been well covered in many
publications. However, there have been attempts to
compare the Spitfire, Hurricane, and Bf109 on a qualitative
basis and a somewhat confused picture has resulted. For
example, it has been said that the Hurricane shot down
many more German aircraft than did the Spitfire. Also,
it is sometimes suggested that the Hurricane was more
valuable, since it was easier to fly, more tractable on the
grass airfields with its wider-track undercarriage, and was
less susceptible to battle damage than the Spitfire.

There is no doubt that there were more Hurricanes than
Spitfires in service (average total strength: 461 to 295; in
11 Group 243 to 137), and therefore the Hurricane would
be expected to have shot down more German aircraft.
However, a statistical analysis of the strengths, RAF
claims, and losses on both sides, shows some interesting
results. The following figures were obtained in examining
the results of the Spitfire and Hurricane only, and ignoring
other British aircraft and the anti-aircraft gun defences:
* In the period, July 1 to September 30, the average
  Spitfire strength was 38%, Hurricane 62%.
* Spitfires shot down 43% of all the German aircraft des-
  troyed in combat, whereas Hurricanes shot down 57%.
* During July and August, Spitfires shot down 49% of the
  Bf109's of the Luftwaffe destroyed in combat. After
  August, when Spitfire squadrons were encouraged to

take on the Bf109's (leaving the bombers to the Hurricanes), the percentage increased. Taking the entire Battle, Spitfires shot down 54% of all the Bf109's that were lost in combat.

* Despite the fact that more Spitfires than Hurricanes were engaged in combat with the Bf109's, and were usually outnumbered by 4:1, Spitfire combat losses were 39%, against those of the Hurricane at 61%— almost exactly proportional to their relative strengths.
* In examining training accidents, the accident rate for both Spitfire and Hurricanes was *identical*: 4% written-off, and 3% repairable.

In other words, the scoring *rate* for Spitfires was much higher than that of the Hurricanes, especially where the Bf109 was concerned, and Spitfires were no more vulnerable than Hurricanes in either combat or in training. Finally, it is interesting to examine Spitfire versus Bf109 and Hurricane versus Bf109 losses, where it is known that the two aircraft were in combat together:

Spitfire versus Bf109 : 219 to 180 lost
Hurricane versus Bf109 : 272 to 153 lost

One may be criticised for such an unemotional examination of the Battle, but the statistics throw some light on the eternal Spitfire/Hurricane controversy.

In trying to sort out which squadrons were the most successful, it is necessary to realise that fighting conditions varied throughout the Battle and the locations of the individual squadrons made a difference. On the basis of claim-to-loss ratio, 234 Squadron was the most successful of all units, claiming 7.7 aircraft shot down for every one Spitfire lost. Against the Bf109, both 41 and 603 Squadrons were pre-eminent and, against other German aircraft, 609 Squadron was very successful.

After the Battle the Spitfire became the favourite fighter aircraft and was developed through the succession of Marks II, V, VIII, IX, and XIV. These aircraft have been described in considerable detail elsewhere, but the other versions, comprising high-altitude fighters and photographic-reconnaissance types, have been less publicised. Yet their development was vital to 'improvement of the breed' and for the overall War-effort.

An interesting photo, since it shows one of the special long-range Spitfire IIA aircraft with a 40 gallon fixed external fuel tank on the port wing. A number of these Mk.II's were modified to Type 343 standard in 1941 to provide escorts to the bombers attacking the Brest peninsular. This aircraft, LZ-C, is of 66 Squadron, and the pilots found the aircraft to have very poor handling characteristics.

Spitfire VA, W3119, flying in the United States, March 1942. This aircraft went to Wright Field in the summer of 1941, and provided much data on handling characteristics which was useful in the development of later American fighter aircraft.

Spitfires at Dispersal

Above: Taxiing the Spitfire was tricky since the nose obstructed the pilot's view. Ground handling was also improved by having a man at each wing tip to steady the aircraft over rough ground, and for assisting in turns. Often, the ground crew would ride on the wing-tips as shown in this photo of a Spitfire VB, SH-E, of 64 Squadron returning to dispersal at Hornchurch in the winter of 1941-42.

Below: Taxiing more sedately is BM271, *Kenya Daisy*, a Spitfire VB of 165 Squadron at Gravesend in October 1942. At the time, this aircraft was marked SK-E, but soon afterwards was modified as an LF.VB and served with several of the units at Skeabrae/Sumburgh in the winter of 1943-44.

Above: A photograph full of the atmosphere of the summer days of 1941 when the ''sweeps'' over France occupied many of the Spitfire squadrons. One can almost hear the roar of the Merlin engines as this squadron takes off from Northolt, while others form up in the background.

Right: A quiet, rather homely, portrait of a 129 Squadron Spitfire Vc at Ibsley in May 1943. The aircraft is EE602 (painted over on the fuselage, and in small letters at the base of the fin), DV-V. It has clipped wings, but was not modified to LF. Vc standard at the time. Built by Westlands, it carries the presentation: 'Central Railways Uruguayan Staff'.

Right: This Spitfire F.IXc, MT-J BS546, *O Guarany,* of 122 Squadron appears to have a 'B' type wing. However, it does have the 'C' wing, but with the extra cannon stubs removed, outboard of the 20 mm cannon.

Left: No apology is made for this photo. It is EB-B MB882, a F.XII of 41 Squadron, shown many times before. However, it does show the aircraft in its true element: low altitude defence of the towns on the South Coast. In this case it is over Eastbourne, and the date is April 1944.

Development of the Breed

Left: This is a F.XIVc, DW-D RB159, the C/O's aircraft of 610 Squadron in the Spring of 1944. This aircraft had a long career later with 350, 41, and 416 (RCAF) Squadrons, before being sold for scrap in November 1949.

Right: One of the Spitfire VI prototypes, X4942, is seen here at Boscombe Down in the autumn of 1941. This aircraft featured a very large radiator which was not used on the production models.

Right: Spitfire VI, AB176, the first pre-production prototype at Eastleigh in late 1941. This aircraft was originally earmarked for service trials with 501 Squadron, but it was not sent. Later, in 1942 it was intended that 91 and 421 Squadrons should re-equip with the Mark VI, but neither unit ever received this version, and 616 Squadron was the first unit.

Left: SL574 LF.XVI of the last production batch, built in August 1945. It served with the Empire Air Armament School (later Central Gunnery School) and No 3 Civilian Anti-Aircraft Cooperation Unit. Afterwards it appeared at the Royal Tournament, Earls Court, in 1957.

Development of the High Altitude Spitfire

Above: Spitfire VI, BR579, ON-H of 124 Squadron, North Weald, on a foggy morning in November 1942. This aircraft had an active career, being used on the squadron's first operational sweep on July 28, 1942. It was also flown by Plt Off Kilburn over the Dieppe raid on August 19, claiming one 'probable'. It left 124 in February 1943, and saw service at Skeabrae until the end of the year.

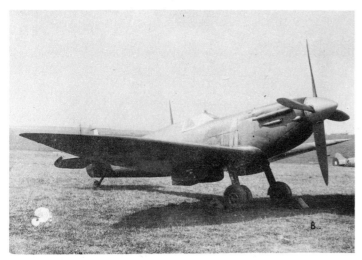

During 1940 the development of high-flying fighter and bomber aircraft came to a head. During the pre-war period between 1932 and 1938 the world altitude record had been pushed up from 43,976 feet to 56,046 feet. All the major powers had taken an interest in the problems of high-altitude flight which required special engine development, ample wing area, and attention to crew comfort, the latter achieved by provision of a pressure cabin.

In terms of military applications, the Germans achieved considerable success, and in 1940 the first Ju86P aircraft appeared over Britain. By this time, the Air Ministry had realised the military significance of high-flying aircraft and had already issued fighter and bomber specifications for such types. September 1940 saw the first flight of the Wellington V equipped with a pressure cabin, and this aircraft provided much useful data for the British aircraft industry.

The Vickers-Armstrongs group had consistently been interested in the problems of high-altitude aircraft, and therefore it was quite natural that Supermarine should follow suit. Early in 1941, the design team under Joe Smith began work on two private ventures, the Types 350 and 351, which were eventually to emerge as the Spitfire VI and VII. Of the two, the Mark VI was to appear first, being an adaption of the existing Mark VB, whereas the Spitfire VII was a new design. The latter was planned around a new Merlin engine with a two-stage supercharger, still under development at that time. However, both aircraft incorporated a pressurised cockpit, and extended wing-tips for the required increase in wing area.

Considering the developmental problems that were

17

encountered, it was quite remarkable that by December 1941 the first Spitfire VI came off the production line, and the Mark VII prototype, AB450, followed soon after in April 1942. That month also saw the first flight of the Spitfire IX, which had great potential for high-altitude defence; and on the 22nd the first Mark VI, BR174, was delivered to 616 Squadron. At that time the unit was stationed at Kingscliffe, Northants, and the pilots attended courses at the A. & A.E.E., Boscombe Down, to be familiarised with the Spitfire VI and the problems of high-altitude flying.

However, during that period there was no real threat of high-altitude attack, and Fighter Command was unfamiliar with the special operational requirements of that form of defence. It was therefore a rather frustrating period for the pilots of 616 Squadron. The first combat involving a Spitfire VI was over Leicester on May 25 against a Do217 which could only be claimed as damaged. At Scampton on the next day, BR172 crashed and was written-off. Already the non-sliding cockpit canopies (initially required for proper cabin sealing) were unpopular, and on early practise formation flights the pilots removed the canopies. In mid-June a temporary ban on operations below 20,000 feet was instituted because of excessive cockpit heating—another problem due to cabin sealing.

In July, when most of the cabin problems had been solved, the squadron moved to Kenley, but this was too close to France to allow for the required climbing distance to 30,000 feet plus, when operating on sweeps. However, on the 28th of the month the first joint operation was conducted with 124 Squadron which, operating from Gravesend, had received a full complement of Spitfire VI in the previous few weeks. On the next day it would seem that Fighter Command had recognised the problems of the two squadrons, and both were pulled back, 124 Squadron moving to Debden and 616 to Great Sampford, the satellite airfield.

Prior to the moves, F/L Gaze of 616 Squadron had properly 'blooded' the Spitfire VI when the first Fw190 was claimed as destroyed on July 18, but the first big action was during the Dieppe landings on August 19. Both squadrons were engaged, losing one pilot each, with 616 claiming one enemy aircraft destroyed, and 124 claiming three.

It was at this point in time that the Germans began high-altitude operations of a more serious nature. Almost simultaneously a number of Ju86P and Ju86R aircraft began reconnaissance and bombing sorties over Southern England and Alexandria in Egypt, at heights between 40,000 and 50,000 feet. In England, it was soon obvious that the Spitfire VI was not capable of reaching the required altitudes. On September 5, P/O Hibbert of 124 Squadron stalled his aircraft at 36,500 feet in attempting to attack a Ju86. On the 9th, two Mark VI of 616 Squadron could only reach 38,500 feet after a Ju86 over Clacton—and that was after the pilots fired off their machine-gun ammunition to reduce the weight of the aircraft.

Above: This Spitfire BF273, a Mark IXC, together with BF271, formed the original equipment of the High Altitude Flight at Northolt in September 1942. It later went to 124 Squadron at North Weald. In March 1943 the two aircraft were repainted as BS271 and BS273, and the latter was flown on scrambles on many occasions by Plt Off Prince Emmanuel Galitzine.

Opposite: AB450 the Spitfire VII prototype as it appeared in late 1942 with the High Altitude Flight, Northolt. The cannons have been removed to save weight, and the new camouflage of medium sea-grey and PRU blue is apparent.

Unfortunately, the Spitfire VII was not really quite ready for service, but nevertheless Fighter Command reacted quickly and, in the first week of September, the High Altitude Flight (later known as the S.S. Flight) was formed at Northolt, initially equipped with two specially modified Spitfire IX. These two aircraft, BF271 and BF273, were lightened by 450 lbs, the machine guns and armour being removed. Within two days of the formation of the Flight, P/O Galitzine intercepted a Ju86 at 42,000 feet. During the engagement one cannon jammed and when the combat finished at 44,000 feet, the pilot could only claim the enemy aircraft as damaged.

A special control room was set up at 11 Group for co-ordinating the radar warning system and control procedures and, within a few weeks, the Flight had quite a mixed complement of aircraft. Another Spitfire IX (BR639), the prototype Mark VII, and a Mosquito arrived on September 16. These were followed by a Spitfire VI (BR326) modified to incorporate a liquid-oxygen engine boost system. This increased the ceiling of the aircraft to above 40,000 feet, giving an increase of 40 to 50mph in speed at that height. Finally, the first and second production models of the Spitfire VII (BS121 and 142) arrived in the last week of the month. By now the inclement autumn weather had arrived and none of the aircraft had a chance to establish their worth, the last interception being on October 2 but, on this occasion, the enemy aircraft turned away before contact was made.

As is now well-known, the Special Performance Flight

at Aboukir in Egypt had more success with their special Spitfire Mark V aircraft and shot down several Ju86, but at the expense of considerable strain on the pilots. Nevertheless, in the winter months, the Northolt Flight was to gain very valuable experience in solving some of the operational problems of the high-altitude defence. For example, there were problems with leaking pneumatic systems, special dietary requirements for the pilots, and difficulties with armament (cannon firing at 44,000 feet caused a large vapour cloud and instrument flying was required for half a minute). Another requirement was fuel refrigeration, there were radio and electrical problems, and even the tyres became deflated on one Spitfire VII after a flight to 44,000 feet! Much of what was learnt was later applied to both the military and civil jet aircraft that were to follow in later years.

Meanwhile, in the winter months of 1942-43, 124 and 616 Squadrons soldiered on with their Spitfire VI's, the latter keeping quite busy with normal patrols and escorts. 124 Squadron were handicapped by numerous moves until finally establishing themselves in January at North Weald. Here they absorbed the S.S. Flight, now made up of one Spitfire VI, four Mark VII, and the two original IX's. These aircraft were kept together in one special flight and, while the remainder of the squadron continued operations on the Mark VI, the special flight detached three Mark VII to a succession of airfields in south-west England at the end of April. Finally, on May 15, F/O Willis in BS142 had the first success at high altitude when he shot down a Fw190. This was one of a pair intercepted at 38,000 feet near Plymouth and in the ensuing dive to 19,000 feet, one was destroyed.

There were numerous scrambles during the summer of 1943 and, although very few enemy aircraft were shot down, the scrambles were very successful because enemy aircraft would often turn back as the Spitfires reached operational altitude. In June, the remainder of the squadron began to receive a new batch of Mark VII and, in July, the pilots received pressure waistcoats and oxygen masks that were really essential for high-altitudes. This special equipment was necessary because it had been found that in the event of cabin de-pressurisation, due to combat damage or compressor failure, it was very difficult to breathe properly above 42,000 feet.

As the Spitfire VI aircraft were replaced by the Mark VII on 124 and 616 Squadrons (the latter re-equipping in the September-December period), they were passed on to the Meteorological Reconnaissance units. In the United Kingdom these were comprised of a number of Flights and Squadrons, the first to receive the Spitfire VI being 521 Squadron at Bircham Newton in February 1943, followed by 1406 Flight at Wick, in April. These units normally employed their Spitfires for obtaining air pressure, temperature, and humidity readings during climbs to 40,000 feet above their respective bases. After much changing around between Flights and Squadrons, and re-equipment with the Mark VII in 1944-45, the two remaining units after September 1945 were 518 Squadron at Aldergrove, and 519 Squadron at Leuchars.

Meanwhile in October 1942, at Aboukir in Egypt, six Spitfire VI aircraft had arrived, but these were soon discovered to be unsuitable for very high-altitude defence. Because no Mark VII were sent to the area, the squadrons in the Mediterranean had to wait until the Spitfire VIII arrived in mid-1943. These aircraft were almost identical to the Mark VII except for the elimination of the pressurised cockpit, but the earlier production models had the extended wings and, apart from pilot discomfort, proved very acceptable for high-altitude operations. In the early days of the invasion of Italy, 92 Squadron employed the Spitfire VIII to cover the naval base at Taranto.

As in England, the adaptable Spitfire IX was also

This view shows the pointed wing-tips of the F.VII to good advantage. The aircraft is EN474, flying over Ohio, USA, in the summer of 1943.

Left: The second production Spitfire F.VII, BS142, in September 1942 just before it went to the High Altitude Flight at Northolt. Points to note are the gloss finish, new wheel hubs, and the Standard Beam Approach (SBA) aerial under the fuselage. In January 1943, it went to 124 Squadron and replaced BR579 as ON-H. On the 15th May, flown by Fg Off Willis, it claimed 124 Squadron's first high altitude victim: a Fw 190.

modified for high-altitude operations, usually at reduced weights, together with local modifications including extended wing tips, and Aboukir-type carburretor intake filters. These aircraft were used by a number of squadrons around the Mediterranean including 32 and 238 Squadrons in Italy, 451 Squadron in Corsica, and 74 Squadron in Egypt. In late 1943, the latter unit was given the important task of providing the high-altitude defence of Cairo during the conferences between Mr Churchill and President Roosevelt. Based at Cairo West and Dekheila, 74 Squadron had a mixture of normal Mark VB and VC aircraft, together with the special Mark IX—which included BS354, MA256, and MA455. No Luftwaffe attacks materialised during the Cairo conferences, and when 74 Squadron returned to England in 1944, some of the Spitfire IX's were passed on to 213 Squadron.

Returning to 124 and 616 Squadrons in England: in September 1943 the two units moved to take up residence at West Malling and Exeter, respectively. Once more, 124 Squadron was involved in special operations when it provided fighter cover during the last day of Operation 'Starkey'. This was a rather long and complex operation which took place between August 16 and September 9, to try and force the Luftwaffe into the air over Europe by prolonged bomber and fighter attacks. It culminated in a combined operation with naval forces which sailed up the Channel to simulate a landing at Boulogne. In this operation an attempt was made to avoid the very unfortunate mistakes of aircraft recognition by naval units during previous landings in enemy waters. This was done by painting black and white stripes on the wing-tips of the aircraft that were to fly over the 'beach-head' and, since this proved successful, the markings were later adopted, in modified form, for the real invasion in June 1944.

By that time, 124 and 616 had been joined by 131 Squadron which received Mark VII's in March of 1944. On D-Day, 131 and 616 Squadrons were both operating from Culmhead giving high-altitude cover over the landing beaches, and often coming down to low-level for ground attack. By now the Spitfire VII was regarded as a standard operational fighter and, with a decrease in high-altitude operations, the pilots of 131 Squadron removed the extended wing-tips. On June 20, the new 90 gallon drop-tanks were fitted and, for the first time, really long-range operations could be conducted. 124 Squadron was based at Bradwell Bay during the invasion and, being at a more easterly location, the unit saw less action before re-equipping with the Spitfire IXE in July.

In that same month, 616 Squadron, with twenty-seven months of hard-won experience behind it, took delivery of the first Meteor jet-fighters, to begin a new era in the RAF. This left 131 Squadron to continue with the Spitfire VII, and they were kept very busy for several months providing escort cover for Lancasters on day bombing, and for Dakotas and Liberators on the Arnhem operation. On October 30, 1944, 131 Squadron flew their last operation, their aircraft being taken over in mid-November by 154 Squadron on reforming at Biggin Hill. However, only a few months later this unit changed over to the Mustang.

Considering that only one hundred Spitfire VI, and one hundred and forty Mark VII had been built, it is quite remarkable how much the aircraft had been used, and how much had been learnt through the development and operational use of the two versions. As will be described later, the aircraft were also used to defend the naval base at Scapa Flow and, in addition, the experience of high-altitude operations was put to great use in the development of the photo-reconnaissance Spitfire.

The end of the War was not the end of the Spitfire VII, for besides its use on Meteorological work, it was employed at several Air Gunnery Schools, notably No 2 at Dalcross and No 11 at Andreas, both in Scotland. However, by 1947 they had all been withdrawn from service and most of the survivors were scrapped. Even then, a few remaining examples (including EN285 which had served on the S.S. Flight at Northolt, and with 124 Squadron) were sent to Shoeburyness, where in 1948-49 they ended their useful lives as ground targets for anti-aircraft fire. The purpose of these trials was for the observation of the effects on the pressure-cabins.

Today, only one Spitfire VII remains in existence and that is EN474. Owned by the Smithsonian Institute, the aircraft is presently in storage near Washington in the United States. It is to be hoped that it will be displayed soon and, in view of its contribution to aeronautical science in Britain, perhaps this unique survivor could be returned to this country for permanent exhibition?

Another Spitfire IXc modified for high-altitude work, this one was used by the Special Performance Flight at Aboukir in 1943, for protection of the Canal Zone in Egypt. It is possible that this was BS354, which was later used by 74 Squadron in the area.

Defence of the Orkney and Shetland Islands

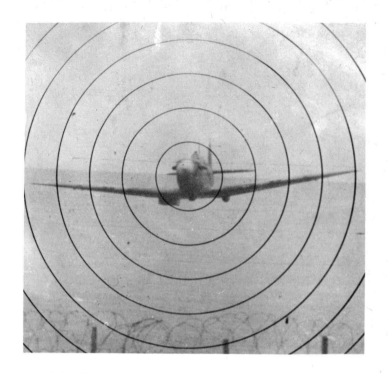

The squadrons in the Orkneys and Shetlands for their enforced 'rests' found them boring and uneventful. However they could prove dangerous, and sometimes sorties ended in tragedy. This Spitfire, a Mark VA of 164 Squadron was on anti-aircraft cooperation near Sumburgh. Seconds after this photo was taken through the Bofors gunsight, the aircraft hit the ground, killing the pilot.

During the War the northern islands of the United Kingdom were of great strategical significance, particularly from a naval point of view. Scapa Flow, in the Orkneys, was the main base of the Home Fleet; stationed at Lerwick, and later Sullom Voe, in the Shetlands, were the flying boats of Coastal Command covering the waters up to the Norwegian coast. At the outbreak of War the fighter defences were stretched to the limit, and nothing could be spared for the far north. As a result, the first attack by the German Luftwaffe on Scapa Flow on October 17, 1939 was virtually unopposed, and the main Fleet was forced to evacuate to the west of Scotland. Various stop-gap air defence measures were instituted involving RAF Gladiators at Sumburgh in the Shetlands, and Fleet Air Arm Skuas and Gladiators at Hatson in the Orkneys. Also, for a short time after the attack, the Spitfires of 41 Squadron were based at Wick. However, it was not until February 1940 that a proper air defence was instituted with three squadrons of RAF Hurricanes at Wick and, as a result, the Home Fleet was able to return in March.

From that moment until the end of the War, there were two main tasks: defence against bombing attacks and against reconnaissance aircraft and, in both cases, the intruding aircraft would come in during daylight either at a very low altitude, or very high to avoid interception. As the Spitfire became the primary home defence day-fighter in 1941 it also appeared in the Orkneys and Shetlands. By this time the main airfield covering Scapa Flow was at Skeabrae and squadrons rotated there, exchanging places with each other during their 3-4 month rest periods from operations in the south of England. Normally, one flight of each unit was detached to Sumburgh and, on occasions, two aircraft would be sent as far north as the airfield at Scatsa for short periods (see map).

Skeabrae had opened in the autumn of 1940, but the first Spitfires to be based there were Mark IIA's which replaced the Hurricanes of 331 (Norwegian) Squadron in November-December of 1941. In the following year, 331

was joined by 132 Squadron at that bleak outpost and, at the end of March, both units re-equipped with the Spitfire VB. In May 1942, 164 Squadron arrived with sixteen Mark VA, being one of the few units to have a full complement of this particular version, and a Ju88 was claimed as 'damaged' on the 31st.

On September 1, the first Spitfire VI aircraft arrived (BR298, 577, and 979), 164 Squadron being the third unit in Fighter Command to receive this type. However, within two weeks, when three more had arrived, they were handed over to 602 Squadron, together with the Mark VA's, the latter being replaced by brand-new Westland-built Spitfire Vc's in October.

The duties of these squadrons consisted mainly of convoy patrols, readiness duties, some army co-operation, and standing patrols. These may have been very 'restful' but, for the pilots, the patrols were very boring and uneventful. The Spitfire VI was mainly intended for 'scrambles' against high-flying reconnaissance aircraft, and the first of these was on September 17 by 602 Squadron, but no contact was made. This was not at all unusual, even when contacts were obtained by Spitfire V's they were often too late, due to the very low approach of the Ju88's, and at the higher altitudes the enemy aircraft would sometimes turn back. More often than not it would be a friendly aircraft that was off track or not identified as such by the local radar stations at Gaitnip, Nether Button, and Thrumster.

From mid-1942 onwards there were many complicated moves by the various flights of Spitfire squadrons changing places between the south of England and the airfields of Skeabrae, Sumburgh, Scatsa, Grimsetter, and Castletown. In November, 602 Squadron transferred their Mark VI's to 129 Squadron at Grimsetter. By this time the Spitfire VI had proved to be an unpopular aircraft and was considered inferior to the Mark V in all respects, although most squadrons made many brave attempts to get to '40,000 feet or bust!' In January 1943, a pilot of 129 Squadron

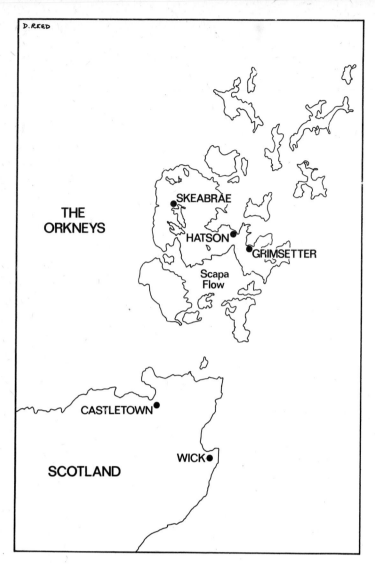

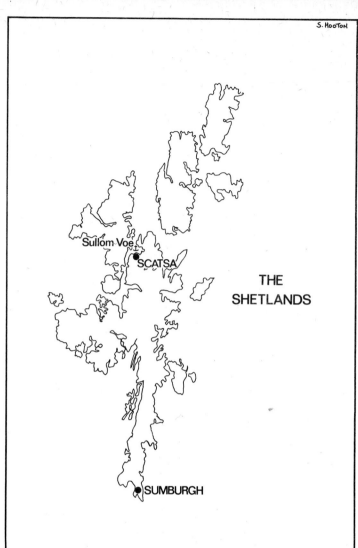

managed to reach 41,000 feet during an air-test, and this was probably a record for any Mark VI in squadron service.

The average unit strength of these Spitfire VI was nine aircraft and in 1943 they were passed on to 234, 66, 313 and 310 Squadrons, in that order, together with some rather tired Mark VB, and the VC aircraft. For example, VC EE661 was flown by 66 Squadron as LZ-R, and by 310 Squadron as NN-V.

Finally, in the last weeks of September, the Mark VI's were taken over by 'A' Flight of 504 and 'B' Flight of 118 Squadrons based at Castletown and Peterhead, respectively. These two units changed places later in October, but by December the Spitfire VI was no longer in operational use. In the sixteen months it was in service in the north it is almost certain that no enemy aircraft was shot down by this version. Nevertheless, more experience in high-altitude defence had been obtained, and this was not to be wasted.

Meanwhile, in August 1943, the first Spitfire F.Mark VII aircraft had arrived at Skeabrae. Initially, three aircraft were taken on strength and, while allocated to the Station Flight, they were normally attached to the successive squadrons on readiness. On delivery of the aircraft, 312 (Czech) Squadron was based at the airfield, but neither

this squadron, nor 'A' Flight of 118 Squadron which followed, ever used the aircraft for operations. However, in October, 453 (RAAF) Squadron arrived and, at the same time, the Luftwaffe began to take a more active interest in the area. By this date the squadron equipment was established as eighteen Spitfire LF.VB, these having replaced the Mark VC in the previous August-September period. It is not certain whether the three Mark VII ever carried squadron code letters at this time, but they were individually marked: MB763 being 'Z', MB765 'G', and MB828 'Y'.

Sometimes both the Mark V and VII Spitfires would be scrambled against high-flying enemy aircraft so that if the latter dived to avoid the Mark VII's, they would be caught at low-level by the LF.VB aircraft. This technique almost met with success against three 'bandits' on November 7, 1943, when MB765 and 828 intercepted at 37,000 feet, but unfortunately the low-level fighters could not catch up with the enemy as they pulled out of their evasive dive. However, the LF.VB's obtained their first success in December when two (AD557 FU-A, and BL437 FU-K) shot down a Ju88 at a very low altitude.

In January 1944, 453 Squadron was replaced by 602 Squadron and a few more Spitfire Mk.VII began to arrive.

Spitfire Vc, LZ-P of 66 Squadron in the late spring of 1943 on a sortie out of Sumburgh. These aircraft would often provide day escort for the small boats of agents and saboteurs which sailed between the Shetlands and German-occupied Norway.

These aircraft were kept quite busy and were finally rewarded on February 20 when a Bf109G reconnaissance aircraft was intercepted at 32,000 feet and shot down by P/O Blair in MD114, accompanied by F/L Bennetts in MD763. This event caused much jubilation and was repeated on May 30, by which date 118 Squadron had returned to Skeabrae. This time it was a Ju88 at 23,000 feet which fell to F/O Parker in MD118, joined by W/O Taylor in MD122.

Finally, 313 (Czech) Squadron returned in July, but with little further action, the use of the Mark VII's declined and none was used operationally after August. In September, the first Spitfire IX aircraft arrived to replace the LF.Vb and, in October, 611 Squadron arrived for their rest. Had the Luftwaffe mounted their proposed attack on the Fleet at Scapa Flow with the Ju88/Bf109 Mistel composite aircraft in December 1944, there is no doubt they would have received a warm reception from 611 Squadron. In the event, no attack materialised and, with the majority of the Home Fleet leaving for the Pacific during the winter of 1944/45, Skeabrae settled down to a quiet life. Before VE-day, 441 and 329 Squadrons passed through, with 451 and 603 afterwards, but by then it was all over.

Allied Squadrons of the RAF

Left: A very cheery group of Polish pilots surround UZ-T BS459, a F.IXc of 306 Squadron at Northolt, in October 1942. This was a newly-delivered aircraft, but went missing in January 1943.

Left: The Norwegian squadrons of the RAF were very active during the War. This view shows R7127 AH-A, a Spitfire VA of 332 Squadron at Catterick, early in 1942. The Norwegian flag was painted on both sides of the cockpit.

Right: Later in 1942, 332 moved to take up almost permanent residence at North Weald. This Spitfire F.IXc, AH-R BS249, had a long career with 332 and other units, and finally wound up as an instructional airframe, 6452M.

Right: Just starting up in the dispersal area are four F.IXc of 332 Squadron. The squadron badge was carried on the port side of the fuselage only. AH-S MA301, and AH-T LZ919, are both early-production Mk.IXc from the Castle Bromwich factory, and do not have the tropical filter which was standard on all later models.

Left: All these photos of 332 Squadron Mk.IXc aircraft were taken in July 1943. This one shows BS248 leaving dispersal. The large cannon blister on the wing was a feature of the early 'C' wing on the Marks V and IX. Strangely, this particular aircraft remained with its sister, BS249, all through the war and also became an instructional aircraft, 6516M, being sent to the Danish Air Force in 1948.

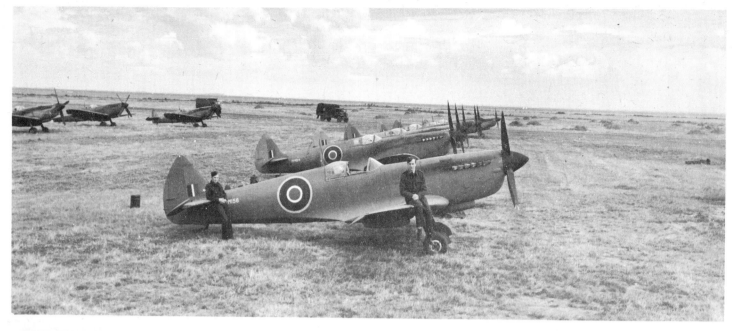

Left: Not previously illustrated, these are Spitfire PR.XI's of 400 (RCAF) Squadron in Germany, August 1945. PM124 and PM156 (foreground) joined the unit early in the year, but shortly after this photo was taken, the unit disbanded. Both aircraft are of the last production batch and have canopy 'blisters'.

Right: Not the best of photographs, yet quite unusual. This is a Spitfire FR.IXc of 414 (RCAF) Squadron of 39 (Reconnaissance) Wing, 2nd Tactical Air Force. These special versions of the Mark IX carried oblique cameras but could fight back, if necessary, with their normal armament. One camera can be seen between the fuselage roundel and the identification letter.

Right: An early production model of the Spitfire LF.XVI, this one belonged to 416 (RCAF) Squadron in Belgium, early in 1945.

Left: Catterick early 1943. 401 (RCAF) Squadron was posted here on 'rest', and this Mark VB, YO-X, is seen at dispersal.

Canadian Spitfires

Right: As far as is known, no photos of 442 (RCAF) Squadron have previously appeared in print. This photo of Y2-K, MK304, shows an engine-change in progress. The aircraft is a LF.IXc.

Left: 403 (RCAF) Squadron Kenley, February 1944, Spitfire LF.IXc. The second aircraft, a Mark VB, is a visitor from the Air Fighting Development Unit.

Right: Two LF.IXc of 442 Squadron taking off from A.L.G. B-4 Berry-sur-Mer, Normandy, August 1944. Both aircraft seen here had quite long careers after this date. Y2-Y,MK464 (foreground), was eventually sold to the French Air Force in 1946. Y2-Z,MK777, later went to 129 Squadron as DV-T and saw service in UK, Norway, and Germany, finally being sold to the Belgian Air Force in 1948.

Right: Engine details of the Merlin XII, starboard side, Spitfire IIA, late 1940. Early-type exhausts, and note the flush mounted oil-tank on the underside of the cowling, in the centre.

Far right: Cockpit and instrument panel of a Spitfire F.21.

'Bits of Spits'

Above: Cockpit and instrument panel of a Seafire FR.47, but with Mark IID Gyro-gunsight removed.

Left: Windscreen details typical of later production models of the Mark VIII and IX. This had the integral bullet-proof windscreen and later, round-type, external mirror (sometimes retrofitted after May 1943). The pilot is wearing the later-type helmet and oxygen mask.

Undercarriage retraction on the Spitfire was fairly rapid but somewhat messy, since one wheel would often disappear before the other. These three photos are very typical and show: AF.VIII, AN-M JF627, of 417 (RCAF) Squadron in Italy.

'Wheels up'

Spitfire PR.XI of 681 Squadron, Palem, India, in 1944-45.

Left: MB952, a PR.XI of the USAAF. This aircraft is seen at Mount Farm in 1944 and is of the 14th Squadron, 7th Photographic Group, 8th Air Force.

Right: Known to Supermarine personnel as *The Narvik Nightmare*, this Spitfire I, R6722, was mounted on Blackburn Roc floats at the time of the Norwegian campaign in the Spring of 1940. Tank tests of models showed rather poor water handling characteristics, so perhaps it was as well that it never flew. However, it makes an interesting comparison with the earlier Schneider racers, and it provided valuable experience for the later Spitfire float-planes.

The drawing here (to 1:72 scale), shows the aircraft as it appeared in 1940. Modellers who wish to make a conversion from a 1:72 Spitfire kit, can use Blackburn Shark floats from the Frog kit, as these were almost identical to those of the Roc. Underside colours were as shown: Black/White wings with silver fuselage. The float colour was basically silver-anodised finish. Roc floats normally had upper surfaces camouflaged in green/grey as shown.

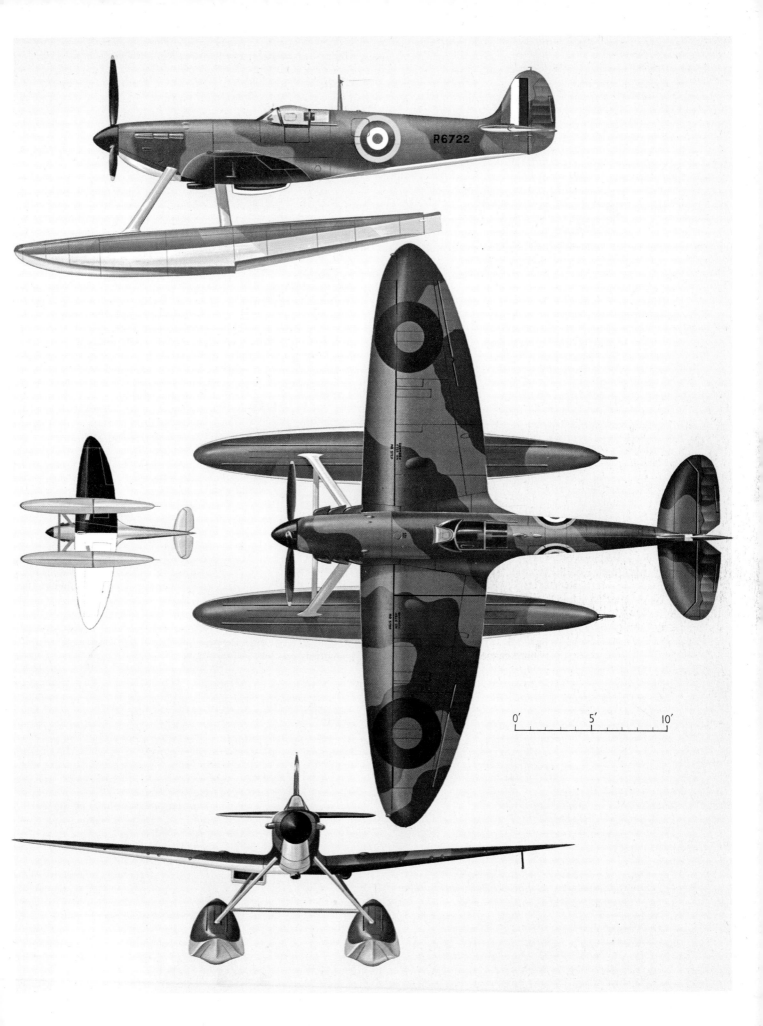

R6722

0'   5'   10'

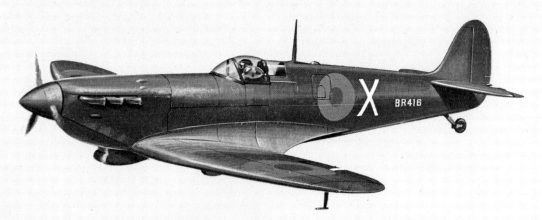

Spitfire PR.IV, BR416. This aircraft was shipped to the Middle East in July-September 1942. It joined No 2 PRU shortly before it became 680 Squadron. During July 1943 it was with 'C' Flight at Nicosia, Cyprus, and flew operational sorties over Greece and the Aegean islands. It later went to 74 OTU in Palestine. The aircraft was painted a special matt-finish dark royal-blue, originally concocted at No 2 PRU. It was fitted with an Aboukir filter, and is shown here as it was at 74 OTU. However, in its previous service with 680 Squadron it would have been identical except for the 'X' identification; this would not have been applied on the squadron. Note the blisters on the canopy and the small + for the pilot (marked on the port blister) to aim against the aileron stripe, when taking oblique photos at low level.

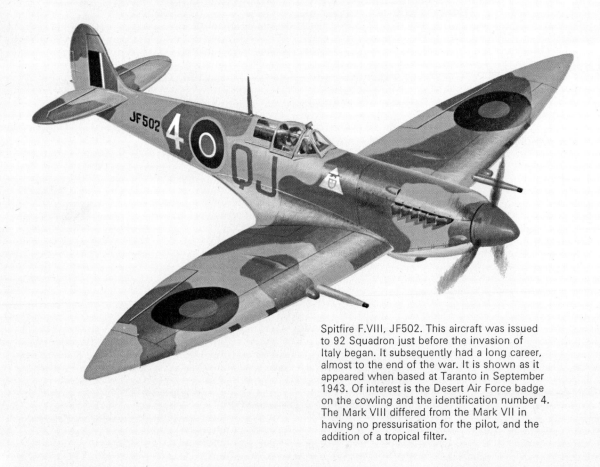

Spitfire F.VIII, JF502. This aircraft was issued to 92 Squadron just before the invasion of Italy began. It subsequently had a long career, almost to the end of the war. It is shown as it appeared when based at Taranto in September 1943. Of interest is the Desert Air Force badge on the cowling and the identification number 4. The Mark VIII differed from the Mark VII in having no pressurisation for the pilot, and the addition of a tropical filter.

Spitfire PR.VII, AR257. Converted from a Westland-built Mark V in January 1942, this aircraft served as a 'dicer' with No 1 PRU and later, 541 Squadron. On March 3, 1943, it was flown on a low-level sortie over Cherbourg by Fg Off G.R. Crakanthorpe (a colourful 'character' on the squadron), and was hit by flak in the starboard wing. However, the damage was not serious and, after repair, the aircraft was transferred to 8 OTU at Dyce, where it was written-off in July 1943. The pink colour was ideal camouflage against gun crews on the ground when flying on overcast days. However, it was not really popular with the PR pilots as they *felt* conspicuous, and also it could be seen clearly against the ground by enemy fighters above them.

Spitfire HF.VII, MB820. This was issued to 124 Squadron in June 1943. On the evening of September 8 it was painted in the special black-and-white wing stripes for Operation 'Starkey'. On the following day, flown by Fg Off Barrit as No 2 to Fg Off Phillips in MB825, it assisted in the destruction of a Fw190 over the Channel at 31,000 feet. The exact configuration of the wing stripes as shown is based on conjecture (hopefully to arouse the interest of those who may know their exact appearance), but the drawing is otherwise believed to be authentic. The upper grey camouflage was that known as Ocean Grey.

The Desert Spitfires

Above: Spitfires were badly needed in the Middle East but none was sent until 1942. The two shown here are the first to be delivered to 145 Squadron at Helwan, May 1942. AB326 is a VB(Trop) and was first shipped from Hull in February, reaching Egypt after flying from Takoradi in West Africa.

Below: Spitfire VB, UF-X EP689, of 601 Squadron, summer 1943. Points to note are the desert camouflage, letters in blue, squadron badge on the fin, and Aboukir filter, plus 'rounded' clipped wing tips.

Above: A unique photo in many ways. In the Tunisian campaign of 1942-43 the Spitfire IX was badly needed to combat the Fw190 of the Luftwaffe. No photo has previously been published of these early Mk.IX arrivals in North Africa. This shows G-R EN455, of 81 Squadron at Souk-el-Arba in April 1943. The aircraft is in desert colours, with light blue undersides. A number of the squadrons in North Africa had unusual code letters during this period, and 81's usual code letters (FL) have been replaced by the single letter 'G', 'R' being the aircraft letter.

Obviously a new delivery, this Spitfire Vc, FT-Z JK101, is that of Sqn Ldr M. Rook of 43 Squadron, NW Africa, 1943. The letters FT ahead of the roundel do not stand out very well and it is probable that they were painted in grey.

Italy 1943

Above: September 1943, 40 (SAAF) Squadron, Taranto. This aircraft is almost certainly WR-R EP688, a modified FR.VB. It has been illustrated elsewhere, but this shows the addition of the name 'BABS' below the windscreen and the yellow wing-leading edge.

Top Right: A Spitfire VIII of 92 Squadron being serviced in Italy, autumn 1943. The Desert Air Force badge can be seen on the fuel tank.

Right: A lecture on the prevention of malaria, 152 Squadron, Italy, 1943. The Spitfire VC in the background is interesting since the yellow cross of the Desert Air Force badge is painted on the lower engine cowling, below the spinner.

A collection of Spitfire LF.VIII's in Burma in February 1945. The aircraft in the foreground, JG253, is marked with the initials of Group Captain H. G. Goddard, while the others are of 155 Squadron, including DG-Q LV735, the fourth aircraft in the row.

The Spitfire VIII in Italy and Burma

Left: 92 Squadron was unusual in that it retained the Spitfire VIII in service in Europe long after the War was over. Therefore, their aircraft were repainted in European colours and MT648, a LF.VIII, is a good example. Seen near Treviso in 1946 it has green-grey camouflage, red spinner and squadron letters (outlined in white), white tip to the rudder, yellow leading edge, and Type C roundels on the upper surfaces together with duck-egg blue band on the fuselage.

Right: These newly-delivered LF.VIII aircraft of 145 Squadron present an immaculate appearance at Canne, Italy, December 1943. The second aircraft, ZX-A (blue lettering) is JF565.

Top right: A short while later this LF.VIII JF503, of 145 Squadron, now presents a much more scruffy appearance as she is serviced and re-armed after the day's operations.

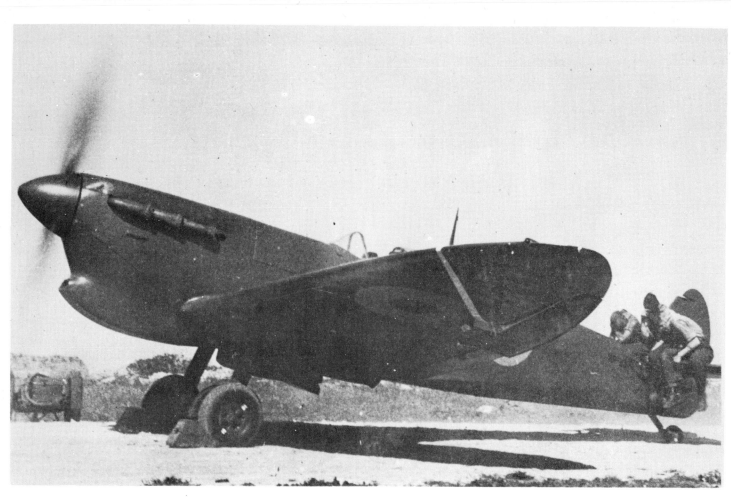

Photo-Reconnaissance Developments

Above: This rear view of a Spitfire PR.IV BP888 shows the strengthening ribs, over the top of the wheel bays, fitted to some aircraft. Also, just visible are the wing-tip vents for the wing tanks, and the sighting stripe on the aileron for the pilot when taking oblique camera photos. The aircraft was used by 543 Squadron in 1943.

Top Left: A PR.VI (Trop) being run up with ground crew on the tail. It is believed that this is BP932 at Malta in 1943, probably with 69 Squadron. It has the dark royal-blue finish common to the PR Spits in that area. The apparent diagonal stripe under the wing is, in fact, a tape indicating that the pilot-head cover is in position.

Left: A Spitfire PR.IV somewhat modified by 103 MU Aboukir. The aircraft had filler applied to achieve a smooth finish, and this was subsequently polished. The wing-tips were extended, and the engine had been specially tuned. It was used by 680 Squadron in 1943 for sorties over Salonika.

By June 1940 the Spitfire was well established it its new role as a high-speed photographic-reconnaissance aircraft. This was mainly due to the early pioneering efforts of Sidney Cotton, the RAE, and the Photographic Development Unit. By the summer of 1940 most of Europe was German-occupied territory, and the Royal Air Force recognised the need for a larger PR organisation with more Spitfires.

In June and July the reorganisation was accomplished, the PDU becoming the Photographic Reconnaissance Unit (later No 1 PRU) with a regular serving officer as its commander: W/C Tuttle. Also, in July, the Air Ministry issued a new specification 15/40 to cover the development of a super long-range version of the PR Spitfire. Considering the many different versions of this aircraft that were to be built or modified to fulfil such a variety of operational roles, it is significant that so few were covered by official specifications. In most cases the development of the Spitfire was prompted by sudden operational requirements in the field, or by far-sighted 'private venture' work at Supermarine.

Cotton's original Spitfires were all modifications of existing fighter aircraft, most of the conversion work being carried out by Heston Aircraft. The new requirement to specification 15/40 was now tackled by the same company. Unlike the earlier attempt by Supermarine to increase the range of the Spitfire I by an externally mounted fuel tank, the new aircraft was to carry its extra fuel internally. This was done by taking advantage of Mitchell's clever wing design and utilising the leading edge of the

wing as an integral fuel tank. Since no armament was to be carried and the aircraft was not intended for combat, this idea was very practical.

The new wings were fitted to two existing airframes, P9551 and P9552, to produce the Spitfire D; and, at the end of October, F/O Millen flew the first operational sortie in P9551, now nicknamed 'The Bowser'. The aircraft was airborne for 5 hours and 25 minutes, and the first reconnaissance cover of the German Baltic ports was obtained. Further flights were made with this aircraft, including some from Malta over Italy, until it was lost on a sortie to Genoa in February 1941. Despite this, the Spitfire D was a great success, and in January of that year Supermarine began small-scale production of this version, based on the Heston drawings. During the summer the Supermarine design team began their own production drawings and finally, in August, the first Type 353 Spitfire PR.IV, AA781, was delivered to No 1 PRU.

At this point the designation of these aircraft should be clarified. When the Type 353 was being designed, the Spitfire VA and VB fighters were in production and the 'C' wing was almost ready. Since the new PR aircraft was very similar to the Mark V, but had the new wing, it was rather conveniently designated the Mark VD. By the summer of 1942 there were three versions, differing in their camera installations:

Opposite: PL775 'A', is a rather normal Spitfire PR.XI of 541 Squadron, Benson, June 1944.

Spitfire V D1 Camera fitment type 'X', one oblique camera for low-level 'dicing'; eg AA784, used by No 1 PRU, later 542 Sqn.

Spitfire V D2 Camera fitment type 'W', two vertical cameras for medium-altitude; eg AA806 of No 1 PRU, later 543 Sqn.

Spitfire V D3 Camera fitment type 'Y', one vertical camera for high-altitude; eg BP922, of No 1 PRU, later 541 Sqn.

Later, in 1943, when the role prefixes were introduced and the original Griffon-powered Spitfire IV was redesignated as the Mark XX, the Mark V D aircraft were, in turn, redesignated as the PR.IV. In an attempt to prevent further confusion, the latter Mark number will be used throughout this text.

By March 1942, over one hundred Spitfire PR.IV had been built, and deliveries could be made to the Middle East where they were desperately needed to replace the vulnerable Hurricanes that had been used since 1940. In Malta, 69 Squadron took delivery of their first aircraft, AB300, which was used operationally over Sicily for the first time on March 15. Two days later, No 2 PRU, at Heliopolis in Egypt, received their first three: AB312, AB421, and BP904. Both units were delighted with the new aircraft which was considered 'infinitely the better machine' when compared with the Hurricane. More

Spitfires arrived, and on the 29th, F/L Pearce of No 2 PRU flew their first sortie over Greece, in BP883.

As in Britain, the stress on high-altitude operations (both fighter and photo-reconnaissance) was to result in all sorts of problems and required alterations to the aircraft. No 103 MU at Aboukir modified many Spitfires and played a large part in the success of No 2 PRU. Extended wing-tips and engine modifications enabled the PR.IV to fly even higher. The unit also fitted their special dust filters, and applied special finishes and camouflage. An early problem was discovered when BP882 burst its wing fuel tanks after standing in the sun. This was caused by fuel expansion, and was remedied by the installation of vent-pipes mounted at the upper wing-tip surfaces. Thereafter, all the PR Spitfires with wing-tanks had a tendency to spout like whales when taxiing out with a full load! It was also found necessary to keep the fuel tanks cool on the ground to prevent the petrol boiling after a climb to altitude. In England, this problem was remedied by the High Altitude Flight with the use of a refrigeration unit to cool the petrol in a special bowser. In addition, wet blankets or sacking were applied to the aircraft tanks when parked at dispersal, and this technique was also used in Egypt.

In October 1942, No 3 PRU in India collected two PR.IV's and the first operational sortie was flown on the

The rather rare, but useful PR.X. This one is SR396 which flew on its first sortie on June 12, 1944. Flown by Plt Off Dearden of 542 Squadron it was flown over France on a 3 hour sortie. It would have had invasion stripes by that date, over its light grey gloss finish

Rear view of the Type 389 Spitfire PR.XIX, RM632. Noticeable, are the different skin and rivet lines on the upper surfaces of the wing, as compared with fighter Spitfires. This aircraft went to 542 Squadron and on June 6, 1944, was flown on its first operation by the indefatigable Crakanthorpe (by then a Flt Lt).

Opposite: PS888 a Type 390 Mark XIX of 81 Squadron Malaya, 1954. This aircraft originally served with 542 Squadron in 1945, and then went into storage. Later it was flown out to Malaya in December 1950 and flew the last operational sortie of a Spitfire in the RAF: April 1, 1954. It was sold to the Thai Air Force in June 1954.

19th. During this period three PR.IV's were also being operated in Russia by a special detachment of No 1 PRU at Vaenga, near Murmansk in the Arctic. In the following month others were in service with No 4 PRU in North-West Africa. The paramount need for the best possible photo-reconnaissance coverage had led to the world-wide use of the Spitfire PR.IV and, in many cases, it preceded the fighter versions in operational service.

The Spitfires in Russia had been sent to keep a watch on the *Tirpitz* and the German Fleet, lurking in the fiords in the northern part of Norway. The presence of these ships had previously contributed to the disaster to convoy PQ17 taking supplies to Russia via the Arctic route. To prevent a similar occurrence to convoy PQ18 and QP14 (the return voyage of the remains of PQ17), it was therefore necessary to maintain a close watch on the anchorages of the German Fleet. Three PR.IV aircraft were flown to Vaenga, via Sumburgh, on September

1/2. On the 9th, one aircraft was damaged on the ground during an attack by the Luftwaffe, but on the 11th the first two successful sorties were flown. Sgt Hardman arrived in a new replacement aircraft on the 19th, photographing the Swedish-Finnish border area on the way. Other sorties were subsequently flown over the Norwegian fiords but, on the 27th, P/O Walker failed to return. After a final successful sortie on October 15, the aircraft were handed over to the Russians, and the pilots returned to the UK by ship.

The period between October 1942 and February 1943 saw the formation of many new PR squadrons out of the original Photographic Reconnaissance Units. The first reorganisation was at No 1 PRU when, on October 19, fifty-two Spitfires were distributed between 541, 542, and 543 Squadrons. Each squadron received more than a dozen PR.IV and three or four PR.VII.

The Spitfire PR.VII was a special version modified by

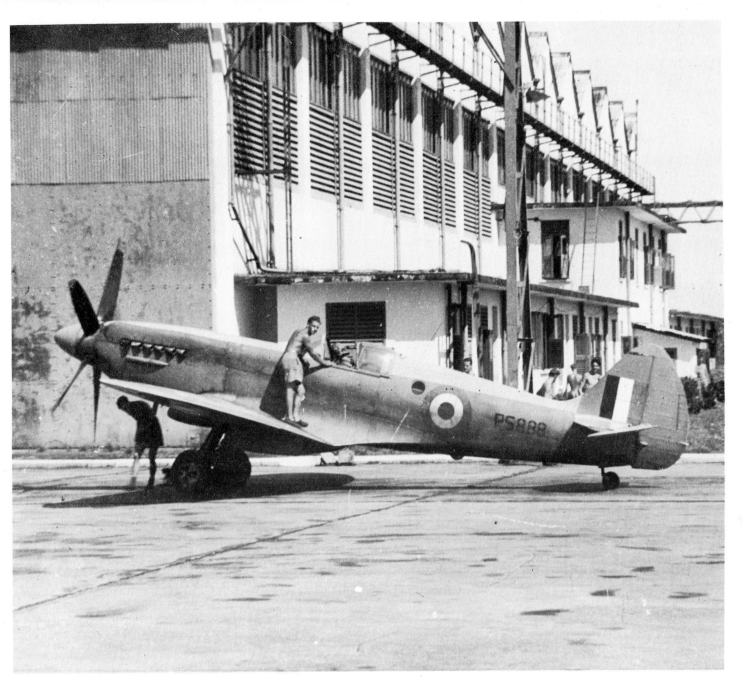

Heston Aircraft from Mark V airframes, and it was originally known as the Spitfire G, or VG. The aircraft was intended for the low-level 'dicing' role and carried eight guns, together with one oblique camera. During the summer of 1942, Supermarine had designed a replacement for the PR.VII and this was to emerge as the PR.XIII. More than two dozen were converted from Mark V and PR.VII airframes by Heston Aircraft, the first aircraft being X4615 which went to Heston in September. (Airframe L1004, often quoted as being the prototype Mark XIII, was not modified until February 1943 and probably carried the 'P' marking from an earlier date.) The new aircraft also carried armament and an oblique camera, but differed from the earlier PR.VII by having a low-altitude Merlin 32 engine and only four guns.

The first Spitfire PR.XIII to enter service was AD354 which arrived at Benson on April 21, 1943, and within a few days 541 and 542 Squadrons had a total of five air-

craft. These aircraft have never received much publicity, and the reason would seem to be that they saw no operational use. However, there was one notable exception. On October 19, 1943, the German ship *Strasburg* of 10,000 tons had been hit by Beaufighters and was beached on the Dutch coast near Ijmuiden. To ascertain the extent of the damage a low-level 'dicing' sortie was required, and the next day F/L Aston of 541 Squadron set off from Coltishall in a Spitfire PR.XIII, AR319, to photograph the ship. As he approached Ijmuiden at top speed he saw a large number of fishing-boats surrounding the *Strasburg*. However, much to his consternation, the 'fishing-boats' turned out to be flak-ships! Despite a hail of fire he managed to obtain excellent photos, although his aircraft was hit several times, one shell hitting the canopy and passing within a fraction of an inch of his head. On returning, Aston had to carry out a 'dead-stick' landing at Luton.

Apart from this brief moment of glory, the Mark XIII's

were only used as trainers, proving most useful for gunnery and aerobatics. No 541 and 542 Squadrons used the type until the summer of 1944, and 543 Squadron had one aircraft until the unit disbanded in October 1943. Also, from late December 1943, No 4 and 400 (RCAF) Squadrons each used three PR.XIII for a few months, during their conversion from Mustangs to the Spitfire PR.XI.

The Mark XI largely replaced the Spitfire PR.IV in many squadrons during 1943, but one unit continued to use the older aircraft for operations until the summer of 1944. This was the special PR detachment at Gibraltar. Since 1942 this unit had been flying reconnaissance sorties over Spain and Spanish Morocco to keep an eye on the airfields and ports, in case they might be extensively used by the Germans. In October 1942 the detachment came under 544 Squadron but, a year later, was transferred to 541 Squadron.

The sorties over Spain and Morocco were very varied, ranging from 'dicing' over the coastal ports to high-altitude flights. Many of the latter sorties were carried out to the limits of range and endurance. In May 1943, Spitfire PR.IV, BS492, carried out a flight of 1,375 miles over northern Spain. In August, BS491 was airborne for a record six hours, going as far north as Bayonne in France before returning to Gibraltar with only two gallons of fuel

remaining. Considering that the Mark IV never carried drop tanks, these flights were quite remarkable.

In Egypt, 680 Squadron was formed out of No 2 PRU in February 1943 and, until August, operated three Spitfire VI aircraft. These were BS106, BS133, and BS149, which had gone to the Middle East for high-altitude defence. However, with the attraction of the pressure cabin, they were subsequently modified by 103 MU as photo-reconnaissance aircraft. For this purpose the guns were removed and a F.8 camera was mounted vertically in the rear fuselage. As before, the Mark VI was not very popular, and 680 Squadron used them mainly for communications duties, although a number of sorties were carried out over Greece and Crete in April and May 1943.

The necessity of a pressure cabin for high-altitude PR sorties had been recognised by Supermarine and, in the late spring of 1942, the company had designed the Spitfire Type 362 Mark X. However, it was not ordered into production, and the next PR Spitfire to enter service was the PR.XI. Initially, these aircraft were converted from Mark IX airframes, the first example being BS338 of 541 Squadron which carried out a sortie over Boulogne on November 30, 1942. Within a short while the new PR.XI was in full production. The aircraft was a great success, being used by all the PR squadrons in England, the

Above: The three Spitfire PR.XI aircraft bought by the Royal Norwegian Air Force after the War. Between 1949 and 1954 they were used by No 1 Photo-reconnaissance Wing (code letter ZB) at Gardermoen.

Left: PR.XIX, PS890, seen here performing a low-level 'beat-up', shared a similar career to PS888. It also went to Thailand, but was subsequently presented to Ed Maloney in California by the King of Thailand. The aircraft is now on display at the 'Planes of Fame' Museum at Buena Park.

Mediterranean, and the Far East. In avoiding interception, the high speed and altitude performance of the Spitfire XI proved most useful. For example, in November 1943, 541 Squadron flew seventy-two sorties, forty-two percent of these being at altitudes in excess of 36,000 feet. However, the strain on the pilots was quite severe, being cramped in a tiny unpressurised cockpit for four or five hours at a time. Medical problems of fatigue, the 'bends', and stomach pains were a constant worry. In February 1944 the pilots of 541 and 542 Squadrons received pressure masks and waistcoats, but the real answer was the Spitfire PR.X with its pressure-cabin. In that same month Supermarine were instructed to resurrect the Mark X design and, as the Type 387, sixteen were built during April and May. They were quickly rushed into service with 541 and 542 Squadrons and remained in use until the summer of 1945. It is rather unfortunate that the Spitfire PR.X has tended to be written-off by aviation historians, and even its pressurised cockpit has been dismissed as an 'unnecessary luxury'. The fact is, that despite the small number built, it was very heavily used until supplanted by the PR.XIX at the end of the War.

The first operation by a Spitfire PR.X was carried out by 541 Squadron on May 11, 1944 when MD193, accompanied by a Spitfire PR.XI, flew a special sortie over the

Splendid underside view of a PR.XIX of Flottilj 11 of Flygvapnet. The fuselage camera ports are clearly visible. The blisters under the wings, near the retracted wheels, are housings for the wing fuel-tank booster pumps.

fortifications along the French invasion coast. 542 Squadron flew their first operation with a PR.X, MD198, on May 24 over Bayeux. From June onwards, both squadrons maintained an average strength of four or five aircraft in constant use.

Coincidental with the introduction of the PR.X, came the new Spitfire PR.XIX. This was initially a 'panic' conversion from the Griffon-powered F.XIV fighter, and Supermarine built twenty-two as the Type 389 in April and May 1944. These aircraft, RM626 to RM647, did not incorporate the pressure-cabin, but this was built into the Type 390 which followed and entered production in November 1944. The Type 390 saw limited operational service before the end of the War with 16 Squadron of the 2nd TAF. (It is rather interesting to note that Spitfire production did not always follow the serial allocation order. In the case of the PR.XIX, the order of production was the RM batch, followed by the Type 390 in the PS batch, finishing with the PM series.)

The first operational use of the Type 389 PR.XIX was by 542 Squadron on May 24, when S/L Ball flew RM628 on a sortie over Le Havre. No 541 Squadron followed suit on June 15, when S/L Saffery took off in RM633 for a sortie over the Ruhr but had to ditch in the Channel due to a propeller failure. By October, 541 Squadron was very busy over Germany using the Spitfire X, XI, and XIX, as well as three special Mustang III's. During this month F/L Garvey was awarded the DSO for two very notable actions. On the 6th, flying in PR.XIX RM637, he was attacked by two Fw190 near Koblenz. By skilful evasive action, spiralling down to the tree-tops, he forced one of his attackers to crash into the ground. Next day, on another sortie in the same aircraft, he ran into heavy flak which severed the elevator trim-tab cables and partially jammed the elevators. Despite these difficulties he completed the photography and returned home, maintaining attitude control with the throttle.

Meanwhile, since August, 542 Squadron had been experimenting with forward-facing oblique cameras mounted under the wings of their PR.XIX's. Eventually, a plan evolved to use these aircraft for special low-level operations inside Germany. To be able to navigate in bad weather the aircraft would formate on a Mosquito aircraft carrying GEE equipment. To conserve fuel and avoid interception, the two aircraft would fly out at high altitude. When approaching the target the Spitfire would then dive to low altitude for the photographic run. After some practise, the first operation was carried out on December 17, 1944. On this occasion F/L Clark, in RM638, photographed targets at Hannover after diving down at 4000 feet per minute from his Mosquito escort.

Of the twenty-two Type 389 PR.XIX aircraft, five were flown to Italy where they were used by 682 Squadron during the winter of 1944/1945. These Spitfires were well received by the pilots. Not only did they help in evading the Luftwaffe Me262 jets during sorties over Austria, but they could out-pace the USAAF P-51D Mustangs in mock combat and races.

At the end of the War the first Type 390 PR.XIX aircraft had just reached 681 Squadron in the Far East, and the type was subsequently used for a number of years in many areas of the world. In the hands of the RAF it was used for survey flights over Africa, Germany, the United Kingdom, Western Europe, Malaya, and Hong Kong. In addition it was employed by the Turkish, Indian, Thai, and Swedish Air Forces. The latter ordered fifty reconditioned ex-RAF aircraft in 1948, and these were all delivered between October 1948 and May 1949. They went into service as the S.31 with Flottilj 11 at Nyköping, equipping the Staff Flight and the 1st, 2nd, 3rd, and 5th Divisions. As in the RAF, the aircraft was very popular and even when flown out of Lulea, near the Arctic Circle, they gave no problems in the very cold weather. In 1954 the remaining forty aircraft were replaced by the S.29C 'Flying Barrel'.

It was in the same year that the last operational sortie by an RAF PR.XIX was flown in Malaya, but the type continued in use in England for meterological flights until 1957.

In summary, it may be said that photo-reconnaissance Spitfires were, to quote a modern phrase, the most cost-effective aircraft ever used by the RAF. Together with the high-altitude fighter Spitfires, and in their post-war service, they contributed much towards the peace of the world and the technological advancement of aviation. It is therefore rather unfortunate that the remaining airworthy Spitfire PR.XIX's kept by the RAF have been painted as 'fighters', when their original role was so effective and, really, needs more recognition.

Pastoral scene at Nyköping, with the tail of 31026 visible in the foreground and an aircraft of the 2nd Division beyond (blue spinner tip). In the background is a Ju86 of F.11.

Below: Aircraft No 60 of F.11. This aircraft was ex-RAF PS875,
and was given the Swedish serial 31040. Originally, the tail number
was 40, but later twenty was added to the airframe number of all the
Flygvapnet Spitfires, to give new tail numbers : 60, in this case.
Very noticeable is the Flottilj badge, behind it is the word
SYRGASPÄFYLLING (meaning Oxygen Replenishment Point),
followed by a red cross on a white disc. The tail and fuselage numbers
were yellow. It is believed that the spinner was painted red.
indicating an aircraft of the 1st Division of F.11.

Above: In Italy, a Spitfire Vc of the 308th Squadron of the 31st Fighter Group.

Top left: Another view of PR.XIX 31040, at Nyköping, but with a different coloured spinner, possibly in green, which would indicate the 5th Division.

Below: July 1943 at Membury. The aircraft is a Mk.Vʙ BM181, of the 67th Reconnaissance Group, 8th Air Force, USAAF.

Allies
and Friends . . . . . .

Above: Spitfire VIII aircraft of the 307th Squadron, 31st Fighter Group USAAF, newly delivered from the RAF, at Nettuno, Itaiy, February 1944. These aircraft were used to cover the Anzio beach-head landings.

Top Right: Major V. C. Fields, commander of the 307th Squadron. At this time he had six enemy aircraft to his credit.

Right: A somewhat 'war-weary' aircraft, this is a late-production Mark Vc with the cannon stubs removed, and six exhaust stubs, making it appear somewhat similar to the Mk.IX. This aircraft belonged to either 327 or 328 (Free French) Squadron based at Borgho, Corsica, in the summer of 1944. It bears evidence of previous American ownership, almost certainly the 52nd Fighter Group.

Spitfire F.XIVE of the Royal Indian Air Force in 1945.

1945 to 1957—
The Swan Song

Top Left: A Mark VC of a Turkish Air Force training unit, probably taken after the War. Of interest is the broad-chord, pointed rudder, probably 'cannibalised' from a Mark IX. Also, the star and crescent marking is now carried on the fin.

Left: Another Spitfire VC, posing as a VB, this time 5521 of the Turkish Air Force on delivery in 1943. A bomb-rack is visible below the wing.

Some mention has already been made of the PR Spitfire in post-war service, but the fighter versions also continued for long after the War, but mostly in foreign air forces. In some cases, such as in Egypt, Israel, North-West Africa, and Indo-China, the aircraft were used in combat, but generally the Spitfires were employed on peaceful defence, training, and photographic surveys.

A number of different versions were supplied to Turkey and these generally had long service careers. At least one of the three Spitfire Mk.I that arrived in 1940 lasted until 1950, and the later Mk.V's continued in use until 1951. However, it was in Portugal that the longest service lives were recorded. That country received a number of Mk.VB in 1943, and the last sortie at the training base of Tancos was made in 1955—quite a record.

In British service, the later Seafire III had vindicated itself in the closing stages of the Pacific War. With the British Pacific Fleet, the Seafire squadrons were 801 and 880 in HMS *Implacable*, 887 and 894 in HMS *Indefatigable*. In March and April 1945, during operations off Okinawa, the Seafires of *Indefatigable* had been confined to Carrier Air Patrols but had shot down a number of Japanese aircraft attacking the Fleet. However, the deck-landing

Above: An early production model of a F.XIVE is SG54 IQ-K of the Belgian Air Force. This had been RN215 of the RAF and was sold to Belgium in September 1948.

Top Right: An interesting puzzle picture. This aircraft is almost certainly a Seafire L.IB, not a Spitfire LF.VB. It has clipped wings, six exhaust stubs, later round mirror, and enlarged balances on the elevators, indicating recent modifications. It most likely belonged to the Combined Spotting Pool (a joint RAF, RN, and USN organisation providing gun-spotting facilities during the Invasion), operating from Lee-on-Solent. The code letters, hidden behind the pilot, were probably 4G.

Right: Seafire L.III, PP979, of 807 Squadron, HMS *Hunter*, in the Far East in 1945. SEAC roundels have replaced those painted on in the UK.

accident rate had been seven aircraft in every one hundred landings.

By early May the accident rate dropped to less than two aircraft every one hundred landings. This was due to the fitting of stronger tyres, some changes in Deck Landing Control officers, and replacement of tired pilots with fresh arrivals from 899 Squadron. Finally, the two carriers were together in July and August for strikes against the Japanese Islands. By this time the Seafires had been fitted with Kittyhawk drop tanks which increased their radius of action, and also gave improved deck-landing characteristics—as compared with the normal 'slipper' tanks.

With all these improvements the Seafire became a much more potent carrier fighter and was not restricted only to CAP duties, but flew escort and strike sorties over Japan.

After the War, the Seafire development finally came to fruition in the FR.47 version. This served with two regular squadrons of the Fleet Air Arm, 800 and 804. It was a very popular aircraft as the contra-rotating propellers gave excellent take-off characteristics, a new undercarriage and wheels made landings less treacherous, and the four 20mm cannon gave a good armament. If any weakness was apparent in the airframe, it was at the rear fuselage where the oblique camera ports were fitted. No 800 Squadron was the only unit to use the FR.47 for war-like operations when, between October 1949 and February 1950, they were based at Sembawang, Singapore, for anti-terrorist strikes. Finally, in the autumn of 1950 they were operated

from HMS *Triumph* in the early days of the Korean War. Some strikes were carried out against road, rail, and port installation targets. Junks, suspected of being minelayers, were also attacked. Also, the Seafires provided CAP for the ships operating off the Korean coastline. These were the last offensive operations of any British Seafires, and by this time the RAF Spitfires were very few in number.

One interesting sidelight on the Spitfire was when the Burmese ordered land versions of the Seafire F.15 for their Air Force. The Central Flying School were given the task of training the Burmese pilots in England. It was realised that similar aircraft with Griffon engines were required, and so twelve Spitfire F.21 aircraft were brought out of retirement from 38 MU. Between November 1952 and March 1953 these aircraft were used by 'K' Flight of CFS at South Cerney.

With the last meteorological flights in 1957 and some target-towing in Belgium, the Spitfire gradually slipped into retirement, leaving an indelible mark on history and on aeronautical developments. Very pleasant memories remain in the minds of all who flew the aircraft, and it is still well known to all generations of people around the world.

Above: Seafire F.17, SX351, of 800 Squadron flying over Valetta, Malta, February 1949. The pilot was Lt 'Dizzy' Steer, senior pilot of the unit. It was practise at that time to paint the pilot's and two senior mechanics' names on the starboard side of the fuselage below the canopy.

Top Left: A Seafire F.15, PR479, of the 1st Training Air Group of the Royal Canadian Navy, Dartmouth, Nova Scotia. Since HF radio was fitted, the radio call-sign VG-AAB is marked on the wings and fuselage.

Left: A somewhat rare version: a Seafire FR.17, SX334. A few of this type served with 800 Squadron in 1948.

Above: HMS *Triumph* leaves harbour with the 13th Carrier Air Group on board, in the summer of 1949. The Seafires are FR.47 aircraft of 800 Squadron, 178 in the foreground being VR967 of Sub Lt D. Reid. Note the rocket rails under the wings, and the aircraft number repeated on the leading-edge.

Top Right: Post-war naval aircraft were noted for their very high-gloss paintwork. This early Seafire FR.47 PS951, is a good example. This one was used for conversion training by 800 Squadron at Donibristle in April 1949, prior to embarking on HMS *Triumph*, after her second commissioning.

Right: Downwind leg before landing-on, Seafire FR.47 VR965 shows the configuration with hook and flaps down, hood open, prior to selecting the undercarriage. This version of the Seafire was very popular with the pilots, being considerably stronger than the earlier types, and having no swing on take-off—due to the contra-rotating propellers.

Demobbed Spitfires

Top Left: An early civil Spitfire in North America was this Mark F.24 N7929A. As VN332 it had been shipped to Canada in 1947 for cold-weather trials, and was sold in March 1951. It is believed that it had a short history as a civil aircraft.

Above: Originally developed as the 'Thin-wing Spitfire', the Spiteful was not an unqualified success, and was pre-empted by the jet-fighter. It was capable of a high speed in level flight, but its handling characteristics caused some arguments between Supermarine and the pilots at A&AEE, Boscombe Down. This beautiful photo shows RB520 the 'hooked' Spiteful F.XIV, in 1946, prepared in anticipation of the naval version—the Seafang.

Left: This aircraft, an LF.IXE, had a long history behind it when this photo was taken in January 1962. Originally NH188, it had served with 308 and 416 Squadrons during the War, and afterwards, with the Dutch 322 Squadron in Java. Subsequently, after target-towing in Belgium as OO-ARC, it was later bought by John Patterson in Canada. As CF-NUS it is seen here on an early flight. It now belongs to the Canadian national collection repainted as NH188, with 421 Squadron markings. As CF-NUS it was painted a rather unpleasant 'kingfisher blue' with the 421 Red Indian badge.

Shape of things to come. To perpetuate the memory of R. J. Mitchell and the Spitfire, a museum is being planned in the city of Southampton. This shows a model of the building which will house a Schneider Trophy S.6B racer and a Spitfire, together with models, photographs, and mementos. Organisation is in the hands of the Junior Chamber of Commerce. Funds for the erection of the building are urgently needed, and part of the proceeds of this booklet will be donated. If you wish to subscribe to this worthy project, please address your contribution to *The Financial Organiser, Mitchell Museum, Southampton Junior Chamber (Projects) Ltd., 53 Bugle Street, Southampton.*